For my daughters, Kirsten and Colleen and
for all the loving children who cross my path.
S.R.

To my mother and father.
B.A.

Copyright © 2002 Birds on a Wire Productions, Sutter Creek, CA

Artistic Consultant: Katherine Venturelli, Sutter Creek, CA
Production Consultant: Flynn & Flynn, Folsom, CA
Digital Prepress Production: James Neal

Critiques courtesy of Mrs. A's 2000-2001 Ione Elementary 6th Grade Class

No part of this publication may be reproduced in whole or in part, or stored in a
retrieval system, or transmitted in any form or by any means, electronic, mechanical,
photocopying, recording, or otherwise, without written permission of the publisher.
Brief quotes embodied in critical articles or reviews my be used.

ISBN 0-9722912-0-2

Library of Congress Control Number: 2002093638

Published by Birds on a Wire Productions, Sutter Creek, CA 95685-1972
www.wiredbirds.com

Printed in Hong Kong
All rights reserved

What do you think of when you hear the word love? Do you imagine two grown-ups falling in love, hugging, kissing and acting silly? Well, it's true, grown-ups hugging and kissing is love, but it is only one kind of love. It is ROMANTIC LOVE. Love is so much more!

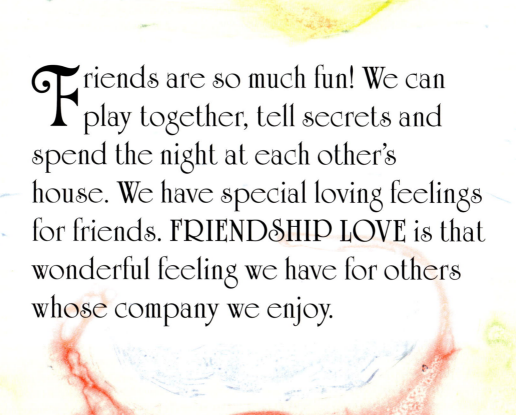

Friends are so much fun! We can play together, tell secrets and spend the night at each other's house. We have special loving feelings for friends. FRIENDSHIP LOVE is that wonderful feeling we have for others whose company we enjoy.

Each of us has a family. They are people who are related to us and care about us. Sometimes our family lives with us and sometimes they don't. They love us very much and we love them too. FAMILY LOVE is a comfortable warm love.

Cats, dogs, birds and other pets may also live with us. They depend on us to take good care of them. We give them food, water, shelter, exercise, medical care and lots of love. PET LOVE is the love we feel for the animals in our lives.

We also care about our home, planet Earth. We want all the plants and animals to be happy and healthy. We enjoy the clean rivers, the lush green forests and the fresh air. EARTH LOVE guides us in taking good care of our planet.

All over the world, there are friends we haven't yet met. Even though we don't know them, we still care about them. We want them to be safe, warm, healthy and happy. We want all people to have the opportunity to be the best they can be. We call this kind of love BROTHERLY LOVE.

But perhaps the most important kind of love is LOVE FOR SELF. When you love, appreciate and respect yourself, all the other kinds of love just happen naturally! So, give yourself a great big hug! You are perfectly wonderful! Be your own best friend. Try new things. Read. Practice healthy habits. Say your prayers. And most importantly, remember that you are loving, lovable and loved!

What do you most love? Is it a hot summer day, a chocolate soda or a really exciting basketball game? Write about what you most love.

Who are your best friends? Describe each one. Tell what you most like about each. What are your favorite things to do with your friends?

_____
_____
_____
_____
_____
_____
_____
_____
_____
_____
_____
_____
_____
_____

Who are the people in your family? Tell about them.

Do you have pets? Tell about the pets you have or the pets you'd like to have.

The earth is our home. What is one thing you could do to help the earth?

All over the world there are kids. How do you think you are like them, and how are you different?

Write down three things you like about yourself. Now write three things you'd like to change or be able to do.